1

Welcome to India

Meredith Costain   Paul Collins

CHELSEA HOUSE PUBLISHERS
Philadelphia

This edition first published in 2002 in the United States of America by Chelsea House Publishers,
a subsidiary of Haights Cross Communications

Chelsea House Publishers
1974 Sproul Road, Suite 400
Broomall, PA 19008–0914

The Chelsea House world wide web address is www.chelseahouse.com

Library of Congress Cataloging-in-Publication Data Applied for.
ISBN 0-7910-6875-7

First published in 2002 by
Macmillan Education Australia Pty Ltd
627 Chapel Street, South Yarra, Australia, 3141

Copyright © Meredith Costain and Paul Collins 2002

Edited by Miriana Dasovic
Text design by Goanna Graphics (Vic) Pty Ltd
Cover design by Goanna Graphics (Vic) Pty Ltd
Illustrations by Vaughan Duck
Map by Stephen Pascoe

Printed in Hong Kong

Acknowledgements

The author and the publisher are grateful to the following for permission to reproduce copyright material:

Cover photograph: Snake charmer in Jaipur, courtesy of Australian Picture Library/David Ball.

AAP/AP Photo, p. 9; Australian Picture Library/Corbis, pp. 18 (left), 30 (5th row); Australian Picture
Library/David Ball, pp. 10 (bottom), 13 (bottom), 21 (left), 30 (1st row, 4th row: middle); Australian
Picture Library/Dinodia Picture, pp. 8, 30 (4th row: left); Australian Picture Library/Jose Fuste Raga, p. 15
(bottom); Australian Picture Library/Woodfin, pp. 27, 30 (4th row: right); Australian Picture Library/Zefa,
pp. 25 (bottom), p. 26 (top), 30 (6th row); Lonely Planet Images/Chris Mellor, p. 23 (top); Lonely Planet
Images/David Tipling, p. 7 (bottom); Lonely Planet Images/Dennis Johnson, p. 21 (right); Lonely Planet
Images/Dennis Jones, p. 20; Lonely Planet Images/Eddie Gerald, p. 14; Lonely Planet Images/Garry Weare,
pp. 6, 18 (right); Lonely Planet Images/Patrick Horton, p. 29; Lonely Planet Images/Paul Beinssen, p. 19;
Lonely Planet Images/Peter Davis, pp. 11, 24, 25 (top), 26 (bottom); Lonely Planet Images/Richard l'Anson,
pp. 5, 13 (top), 22; Lonely Planet Images/Sara-Jane Cleland, pp. 7 (top), 10 (top), 12, 15 (top); Lonely
Planet Images/Troy Flower, p. 28; Patrick Horton, pp. 23 (bottom), 30 (2nd row).

Contents

	Page
Map of India	4
Welcome to India!	5
Family life	6
School	8
Sports and leisure	9
Indian culture	10
Festivals and religion	12
Food and shopping	14
Make *chitchkee*	16
How to wrap a sari	17
Landscape and climate	18
Plants and animals	20
Cities and landmarks	22
Industry and agriculture	24
Transportation	26
History and government	28
Fact file	30
Glossary	31
Index	32

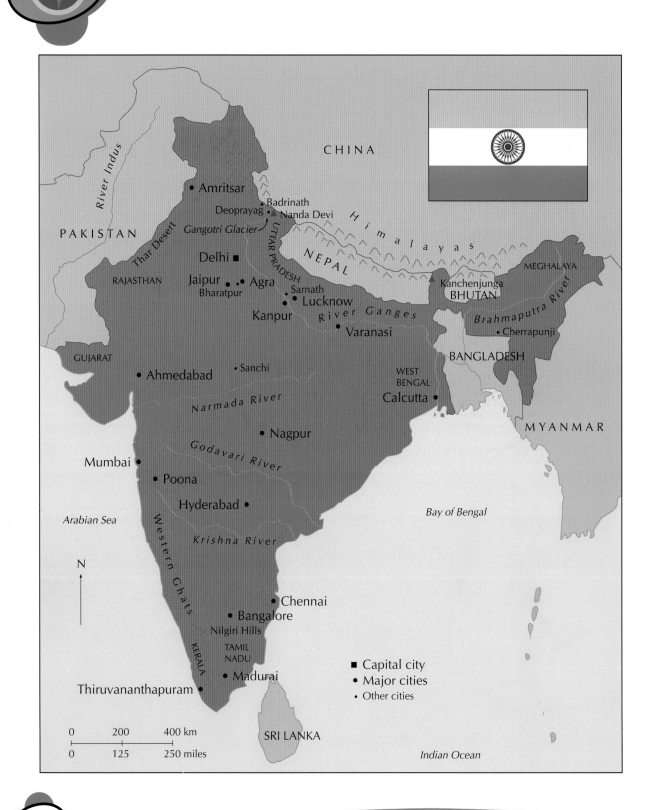

CHINA

PAKISTAN

River Indus

Thar Desert

RAJASTHAN

• Amritsar

Deoprayag • • Badrinath
Nanda Devi

Gangotri Glacier

UTTAR PRADESH

■ Delhi

Jaipur • • • Agra
Bharatpur

Kanpur

• Lucknow
Sarnath

Varanasi

River Ganges

H i m a l a y a s

N E P A L

Kanchenjunga

BHUTAN

MEGHALAYA

Brahmaputra River

• Cherrapunji

BANGLADESH

GUJARAT

Ahmedabad

• Sanchi

WEST
BENGAL

Calcutta

MYANMAR

Narmada River

• Nagpur

Godavari River

Mumbai •

• Poona

Hyderabad •

Arabian Sea

Bay of Bengal

Krishna River

Western Ghats

N

• Chennai

• Bangalore

Nilgiri Hills

KERALA

TAMIL
NADU

• Madurai

Thiruvananthapuram

■ Capital city
• Major cities
• Other cities

0   200   400 km
0   125   250 miles

SRI LANKA

Indian Ocean

Welcome to India!

Hi!

Namaste! My name is Druv. I come from Deoprayag, a small town in Uttar Pradesh, in northern India.

India is a big country, both in terms of size and population. Nearly one-sixth of the world's population lives here! Our neighbors are Pakistan to the west, Bangladesh and Myanmar to the east, and Nepal, China and Bhutan to the north.

Our country is often called a 'land of contrasts'. As you travel around, you will find many differences in landscape, climate, religion, language and culture. We have magnificent mountain ranges, beautiful beaches and hot, dry deserts. Our huge cities are crowded, but many people live in villages in the countryside as well.

Our flag has three horizontal stripes. The orange stripe stands for the **Hindu** people, and the green stripe for the **Muslims**. The white stripe in the middle is for the hope that the two can live together in peace. The blue wheel in the middle of the flag is a **Buddhist** symbol, meaning peaceful change.

Family life

My village, Deoprayag, is a very holy place. It is where two rivers join and become the start of our most sacred river, the Ganges. Every year, **pilgrims** stop here on their way to temples in the town of Badrinath. They bathe in our waters.

Our house is small, but many people live here. My mother and father, my two sisters, my aunt and uncle and their children, and my grandparents all live together. It is the duty of Indian people to look after their parents in their old age.

My father works as a cobbler. People from the village bring him their shoes to mend. My mother and her sister get up at sunrise to collect water from the well and wood for the kitchen fire. They grind wheat to make flour, wash our clothes, keep the house tidy and cook our meals. Once everyone else has been given their food, my mother and my aunt eat their own meal. We believe it is the duty of women to serve others.

This is my village. It is much larger than many villages in the country. Some villages have only one street, and the houses are made of mud and straw. Our house is at the back of the town, near the river.

Here are some members of my family. My mother is holding my new baby sister, Radha.

After school I play *kabbadi* with my friends. *Kabbadi* is a tagging game. One team tries to run from one side of the pitch to the other, while the second team tries to stop them. The last player who is not tagged becomes the winner.

Every day, my mother and the other women in the village collect water from the well. We have no running water in our house. Village life often centers around the well. It is a great place for people to catch up on gossip.

School

Indian children start school when they are five or six. Although they are supposed to stay at school until they are at least 14, many leave before then. Children from poor families often stay home to help their parents on the farm. Boys are more likely to finish school than girls, although this is starting to change.

In many schools, children sit on chairs in rows. They do their school work using slates and chalk rather than pens and paper. In very hot weather, lessons are held outside under a shady tree.

Our school day starts with an assembly. We sing the national anthem and the teacher reads out notices. Then we go inside for lessons. We study Hindi, English, maths, science, social studies, and health and hygiene. After lunch, we play sports and games. We have exams at the end of grades 10 and 12. Some students go on to college or university to study medicine, engineering or agriculture. I would love to be a doctor!

Schoolboys performing exercises during a physical education class.

Sports and leisure

Our most popular sport would have to be cricket! Indian people love both watching and playing cricket. The game was first brought to India by the British army, but we have adopted it as our own. Boys play cricket in the streets after school, and our national team is world-class. Our most famous player is the all-rounder, Kapil Dev. He is the world's highest wicket-taker in **test cricket**.

The games of chess and polo come from India. Polo is a bit like hockey played on horseback. Many people practice yoga, which helps to keep their minds and bodies healthy. All over India, people start the day with a series of exercises called 'salute to the sun'.

Movies are our most popular form of entertainment. Many people cannot afford their own TV sets. Instead, friends gather each evening to watch their favorite programs on their neighbors' TV sets. Other people go to the cinema. Indian movies are very long, and packed with action, music and dancing.

Cricket is our favorite sport. Mohammed Azharuddin is one of our heroes.

Indian culture

India has a rich and interesting past. Wonderful stone carvings, statues and paintings of **Buddha** and Hindu gods and goddesses are found in temples all over India. Many of these were created around AD 400, during the time of the **Gupta kings**.

Many of our dances feature our gods and goddesses. The dancer on the left is Ganesh, the elephant god.

Folk dancers twirl to the rhythm of traditional Indian musical instruments. The main instruments played in India are the sitar (a stringed instrument made from a hollow gourd), and the tabla (a twin drum). Some musicians play the shahnai (an instrument shaped like an oboe), and the sarangi (a stringed instrument played with a bow). Sometimes the sarangi sounds just like a human voice!

Our dances are often based on religious stories. *Kathakali* is a traditional dance style from the south of India. The dancers dress up in elaborate masks and costumes, and paint their faces with bright colors. They use movements of their hands, eyes and feet to tell different stories from our **myths** and legends. Some people use leather shadow puppets to act out the stories.

Our country is famous for its arts and crafts. These include paintings, wood carvings, brass and silver work. Many of the skills used to make these things are passed down from generation to generation in the villages. The people in each region dye and decorate fabrics in their own special way. In Gujarat and Rajasthan, tiny mirrors are sewn into the material. Varanasi is famous for its silk wedding **saris**, which are woven with gold and silver thread.

Billboards advertising 'Bollywood' movies in the town of Chennai, in Tamil Nadu. Our film industry, based in Mumbai, is huge! Over 800 movies are made each year. The films feature brightly colored sets and costumes. There is lots of action, singing and dancing.

Festivals and religion

Religion is an important part of our lives. About 80 percent of Indian people are Hindu, and around 10 percent are Muslim. Other religions followed include Buddhism, Sikhism and Christianity. Family members pray at a little shrine kept at home, or in a temple, mosque or church.

In the Hindu religion, there are many different gods and goddesses. These include the elephant god Ganesh, and Shiva, the Destroyer. Most families choose one special god to pray to. Our special god is Vishnu, the Preserver.

We celebrate many different festivals each year. Our spring festival is called Holi. We burn bonfires to say goodbye to the old year. The next day is Color Day. Relatives and friends get together and splash each other with brightly colored powders and liquids. This is done to scare away evil spirits.

Hindus bathing in the Ganges, the sacred river of India. We believe that the holy waters will cleanse us of our sins (acts we are ashamed of).

Muslim worshippers on the steps of the Jamid Masjid Mosque in Old Delhi. Muslims pray five times a day.

Indian festivals and holidays

New Year	January 1
Pongal (cow festival)	January
Republic Day	January 26
Holi (spring festival)	February/March
Muharram (Muslim festival)	April/May
Independence Day	August 15
Gandhi Jayanti (birthday of **Mahatma Gandhi**)	October 2
Diwali	October/November
Christmas Day	December 25

The Indian New Year is called Diwali. It lasts for five days and marks the end of the monsoon season. People clean and decorate their homes, put on new clothes and exchange gifts with their relatives. Every January, villages in southern India celebrate Pongal, the festival of the cow. Cows and bullocks are decorated with flowers and paint, and then paraded through the streets.

*Children dressed up as a **maharajah** and **maharani** at a festival in Rajasthan.*

Food and shopping

The type of food people eat depends on their religion and the part of India they live in. Many Hindus are vegetarians, although some eat chicken or fish. Because Hindus consider cows to be sacred (holy) animals, we never eat beef. Muslims are forbidden to eat pork.

Tandoori dishes are popular in northern India. Fish or chicken is marinated overnight in a mixture of yogurt and spices. It is then baked in an outdoor clay oven called a tandoor. In coastal areas, fish and rice are popular.

A typical Indian meal consists of spicy vegetables, **dhal**, pickles, crisp **pappadums**, and rice or chapattis (flat bread). We use lots of spices to flavor our food. Chili, coriander, cumin and turmeric are especially popular. A drink made from yogurt, called a *lassi*, helps to keep our mouths cool after all the hot food! We also enjoy drinking hot, sweet, milky tea.

Our meals are often served on banana leaves.

Our meals are served in little dishes on tin trays. Some people serve their food on banana leaves. We do not use knives and forks to eat our meals. Instead, we eat with our right hand. It is bad manners to use your left hand because it is thought to be unclean.

My mother buys fresh fruit, vegetables and spices at the market. On the way there, we stop off at roadside stalls to buy fresh fruit juices and snacks served in fresh banana leaves.

A boy displays his wares at the market.

Market stalls are full of foods with delicious colors and smells.

Make chitchkee

Chitchkee is a vegetable curry. Indian curries can be very hot and spicy! They are usually served with other foods such as dhal, pickles, pappadums, rice and flat bread.

Ask an adult to help you prepare this dish.

You will need:

- 500 grams (16 oz.) mixed raw vegetables (peas, carrots, beans, cauliflower, zucchini, potatoes, pumpkin)
- 1 onion, sliced
- 2 cloves garlic, crushed
- 2 tablespoons curry powder
- 1 tablespoon oil
- 2 tomatoes, chopped
- vegetable stock or water
- squeeze of lemon juice

What to do:

1 Chop the vegetables (except the peas) into medium-sized pieces.

2 Fry the onion, garlic and curry powder in the oil until lightly browned.

3 Mix in the chopped tomatoes. Add enough stock or water to make a gravy.

4 Add the remaining vegetables.

5 Simmer for about 20 minutes.

6 Add a squeeze of lemon juice.

7 Serve with rice, pappadums and plain yogurt.

How to wrap a sari

Women all over India wear a colorful garment called a sari. It is comfortable and cool. A sari has three parts – a tight top, a full-length petticoat, and a long cloth that is wrapped around the waist and draped over the shoulder.

You will need:

- a tight, short-sleeved T-shirt
- a long petticoat
- a long strip of cloth, about 1 meter by 5 meters (3 feet by 16 feet)

What to do:

1 Put on the petticoat and the T-shirt.

2 Pick up one end of the cloth and wrap it around the back of your waist to form a half-skirt. Tuck the edge into the waistband of your petticoat.

3 Fold the loose material across the front seven times like a fan. Each fold should be about the width of your hand. Tuck the tops of these folds into the waistband of your petticoat, and pass the rest of the sari around behind you.

4 Bring the material around to the front, passing it under your arm. Now pull the material up across your chest and over your left shoulder. The end of the sari should fall gracefully down the middle of your back.

Landscape and climate

India is a mountainous country. In the north, you will find the majestic Himalayas – the highest mountains on earth! The word 'Himalayas' means 'abode of snow'. The peaks are so high that the snow on them never melts. They stretch for 2,500 kilometers (1,553 miles) from east to west, forming a wall between India and the rest of Asia.

Pilgrims from Rajasthan travel with their camel herds through the great Thar Desert. Every year, they travel to the camel fair and visit sacred Hindu sites at Pushkar.

The towering peak of Nanda Devi in Uttar Pradesh is covered in snow throughout the year.

The beaches in Kerala on the south-west coast are popular with tourists.

Average temperatures

	January	July
Mumbai	24°C (75°F)	28°C (82°F)
Calcutta	20°C (68°F)	29°C (84°F)
Thiruvananthapuram	27°C (81°F)	26°C (79°F)
Hyderabad	22°C (72°F)	27°C (81°F)

The Sahyadris (Western Ghats) run along the western edge of the Deccan **plateau**. They are covered in rich forests of teak, sandalwood and ebony. The Nilgiri Hills, in Tamil Nadu, are known as the 'blue mountains'. Their soft slopes are covered with grass, flowers, ferns and silvery-blue eucalypt trees. The climate is wonderful, and some people spend the hot summers here.

The vast Thar Desert is in the northwest. This region only receives about 5 centimeters (2 inches) of rain a year. It does not rain at all in some years! But Cherrapunji, in Meghalaya in the northeast, gets about 1,080 centimeters (425 inches) a year. We call it the 'wettest town in the world'. The palm-fringed beaches in the south have a much kinder climate.

The Ganges is our most famous river. It flows for 2,500 kilometers (1,553 miles) from its source in the Gangotri **glacier** to the Bay of Bengal. Its waters are used to **irrigate** farms, and many fish are caught in the river. Hindus believe that water from the Ganges has healing powers.

Plants and animals

There are many different types of plants and animals in India. We have 45,000 species of plants and shrubs, and 81,000 species of animals. However, much of our forest land has been cleared for firewood or farming. As a result, these days you can only see many of our animals and plants in national parks or **wildlife sanctuaries**.

The tiger is our national animal. Tigers were once hunted for sport, but now they are protected. They can still be found in wildlife parks across the country. Elephants, black bears, crocodiles, deer and wild boar live in parks in the foothills of the Himalayas. Rhinoceroses are found in the northern swamps and grasslands. Leopards, hyenas, jungle cats and monitor lizards live in the desert state of Rajasthan.

In India these days, wild elephants can only be seen in national parks.

The Bharatpur Park is one of the finest water-bird sanctuaries in the world. People can travel by boat through the wetlands and see painted storks, spoonbills, cormorants, and white ibis looking after their babies. Every year, rare Siberian cranes make the long journey from the Arctic Circle to their winter home in Bharatpur.

The peacock, with its brightly colored tail feathers, is our national bird.

A snake-charmer from Jaipur with his cobra.

Cities and landmarks

Only 20 percent of our people live in cities. Every year, however, more people arrive from the country looking for work in factories and industries. Our cities are growing each year. The three largest cities are Delhi, Calcutta and Mumbai. Delhi is our capital. It is really two cities in one – Old Delhi and New Delhi. In the old part of town, there are narrow streets and noisy bazaars (markets). New Delhi was built mainly by the British. It has public gardens, wide avenues and modern government buildings.

Mumbai was once known as Bombay. The city is built on seven islands that were reclaimed from the sea and joined together. Mumbai is India's center of industry, and the film capital of our country. It is also our largest port.

There are many wonderful places to visit in India. Hindu pilgrims flock to the ancient sacred temples at places like Varanasi, Badrinath and Madurai. Buddhist shrines at Sanchi and Sarnath were built over 2,000 years ago. The Golden Temple at Amritsar has special importance to people of the Sikh religion.

A busy street in Calcutta, West Bengal. Calcutta is one of the most crowded cities in the world. Many villagers come here looking for a better life. Sadly, most end up living in slums, with no running water or proper toilets. Some end up sleeping on the streets.

The Taj Mahal at Agra was built by the Mughal emperor, Shah Jahan, as a tomb for his wife. It is made of white marble, inlaid with semi-precious stones. People call it the Eighth Wonder of the World.

The Red Fort (Lal Qila) is at the heart of the city of Old Delhi. It gets its name from the red sandstone walls surrounding the building. The fort was built in the 1600s by Shah Jahan, who also built the Taj Mahal.

Industry and agriculture

India's economy has improved dramatically in recent years. It is now one of the most important industrial nations in the world. However, many of our people still struggle to make a living, and to have enough food to eat. Our main industries include textiles and clothing, chemicals, transportation equipment, mining, steel and cement. New industries include computer software, telecommunications and space equipment. Smaller industries produce handicrafts such as silk paintings and wood carvings. These are then sold to other countries.

Two-thirds of our people are farmers. Our major crops include wheat, rice, sugarcane, cotton, tea, coffee and rubber. New methods of farming, called the 'Green Revolution', have made life much easier for some farmers. The government has provided funds to irrigate fields and research the best types of seeds to plant.

Many industries in India are based in villages and small towns.

Harvesting rice by hand.

Most farmers have only small plots of land. They plough their fields using bullocks rather than tractors, and do much of the farm work by hand. The farmers grow enough food to feed their families. They sell the rest at the local market.

Most farmers use bullocks rather than tractors to plough their fields.

Transportation

Indian people love to travel. We enjoy visiting relatives and going to weddings, or making pilgrimages to temples and other holy places. Our country is big, so the best way to get around is to fly. However, most people cannot afford to travel by plane, or even by car. Instead, they take the train.

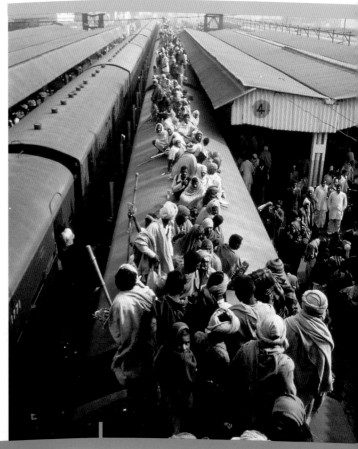

Bullock carts are often used to transport goods in country areas.

Our trains are very crowded, so people stand or sit in any space they can find. They squeeze into the corridor, the floor space between seats, the luggage racks – even on the roof! Many travelers carry their own bed-rolls and buy food for the journey at the station.

*There are many different types of vehicles in India. Look carefully at any traffic jam and you might see cars, trucks, bicycles, **rickshaws**, scooters, motorbikes, bullock carts, buses and carriages drawn by horses, donkeys – or even camels, like this one!*

Our railway system is the largest in Asia, with over 60,000 kilometers (37,260 miles) of track. Most trains are powered by diesel or electricity, but there are still some coal-burning steam trains in service. Express trains run between the major cities. Farmers use the slower trains to take chickens, grain and vegetables to their local market.

Our roads are always crowded and traffic jams are common. Many of them are caused by cows wandering onto the road. There are over 200 million cows wandering around our streets and villages. We are not allowed to move them on. This is because Hindus consider cows to be the most sacred of animals. They are gentle and motherly, and provide us with milk.

Many of the roads in the country are dirt tracks, which become muddy in the rainy season. In desert regions, postal and banking services are delivered by camel.

History and government

The first great **civilization** in India developed around 5,000 years ago along the banks of the River Indus. This is where the name 'India' comes from. About 1,500 years later, these well-planned cities were invaded by the Aryan people. They came from central Asia and Persia.

The Aryans were the first of many groups of people to come to India. They were all attracted by the country's great wealth. In AD 712, Muslim warriors invaded the western borders of the country to spread the Islamic faith. The Muslim **dynasties** were known as the Delhi Sultanate. They ruled India from 1206 until 1526, when the Sultan of Delhi was defeated by Turkish Muslims. These conquerors, known as the Mughals, ruled India for about 330 years. The capital of their huge empire was at Agra. During their rule, they built many beautiful palaces, forts, gardens and mosques.

The Jai Garh Fort overlooking the city of Jaipur, in Rajasthan. The Jaipur Royal House was based here for 700 years. The fort was built for the defense of the town. It has one of the world's biggest cannons on wheels.

The 1600s brought the Europeans. The British, French, Dutch and Portuguese set up trading posts. There was a power struggle between them. In 1757, the British won control of India at the Battle of Plassey. During their two centuries of rule, the British introduced a railway system, many new buildings, and a **democratic** system of government.

After a long struggle, India became an independent country in 1947. In 1950, it became a **republic**. Today, India is the world's largest democracy. The president is our head of state and also commander-in-chief of our armed forces. There are 26 states, each with its own governor, and seven union territories that have less control over their own affairs than the states.

Mahatma Gandhi was one of the leading forces in India's struggle to become a free country. The name 'Mahatma' means 'great soul'. When people marched in protest against the British, he asked them not to use violence, even if they were attacked.

Fact file

Official name Republic of India		**Population** 1,014,000,000	**Land area** 3,287,590 square kilometers (1,269,000 square miles)
Government federal republic	**Languages** Hindi, Bengali, English, Telugu, Marathi, Tamil, Urdu, plus over 1000 local languages		**Religions** Hinduism, Islam, Christianity, Sikhism, Buddhism, Jainism
Currency Indian rupee (Re) 1 Indian rupee = 100 paise		**Capital city** New Delhi	**Major cities** Mumbai, Calcutta, Delhi, Chennai, Bangalore, Ahmedabad, Poona, Kanpur, Nagpur, Lucknow, Jaipur
		Climate varies from tropical in the south, to mild in the north	
Major rivers Ganges, Brahmaputra, Narmada, Krishna, Godavari	**Length of coastline** 7,000 kilometers (4,350 miles)		**Highest mountain** Kanchenjunga 8,598 meters (5,340 miles)
Main farm products rice, wheat, oilseed, cotton, jute, tea, sugarcane, potatoes, cattle, water buffalo, sheep, goats, poultry, fish	**Main industries** textiles, chemicals, food processing, steel, cement, mining, petroleum, machinery		**Natural resources** coal, iron ore, manganese, mica, bauxite, natural gas, diamonds, petroleum, limestone, fertile farm land

Glossary

Buddha	the Indian philosopher Gautama Buddha, whose teachings form the basis of Buddhism
Buddhist	refers to a religion that began in India in 500 BC, then spread all over the world
civilization	the way of life of a particular people or nation
democratic government	a system of government where people vote for who they want to lead the country
dhal	a spicy lentil dish
dynasty	a series of rulers who are from the same family
glacier	a slow-moving river of ice
Gupta kings	kings that came from an Indian family who ruled India for 200 years
Hindu	refers to one of the oldest religions in the world. Hindus worship many different gods and goddesses, and believe in reincarnation
irrigate	to provide water for fields using a series of channels and pipes
maharajah	an Indian prince
maharani	a maharajah's wife or an Indian queen
Mahatma Gandhi	a famous Indian who helped to achieve independence from the British in the 1940s
Muslims	followers of the Islamic religion, founded by the **prophet** Mohammed around AD 600
myths	stories from ancient times that help to explain events
pappadums	thin, crisp bread made from spiced potato or rice flour
pilgrims	people who travel to a holy place for religious reasons
plateau	a large, flat area of land that is higher than the land around it
prophet	a teacher or leader who claims to speak to God or Allah
republic	a country that is ruled by an elected leader rather than a king, queen or emperor
rickshaw	a small two-wheeled vehicle driven by foot or bicycle power
sari	a long piece of fabric that an Indian woman wears wrapped around her body
test cricket	a cricket match between teams from different countries
wildlife sanctuaries	areas of land set aside for endangered animals

Index

	Page		Page
Agra	23, 28	Mahatma Gandhi	13, 29
agriculture	24–25	Mughals	28
animals	20–21	Mumbai	11, 19, 22
		music	10
climate	18–19		
culture	10–11	plants	20
Delhi	13, 22, 23	Rajasthan	11, 13, 20, 28
Deoprayag	5, 6	Red Fort	23
		religion	5, 6, 10, 11, 12–13, 14, 18, 19, 22, 27, 28
family life	6–7		
festivals	12–13	River Ganges	6, 12, 19
films	9, 11, 22		
flag	4, 5	school	8
food	14–15, 16	sports	7, 9
government	29		
Green Revolution	24	Taj Mahal	23
		transportation	26–27
Himalayas	18		
history	28–29	Uttar Pradesh	5, 18
housing	6		
industry	24–25		
Kapil Dev	9		
landscape	18–19